MAR   2017

Creating the Perfect
Wood Finish
with Joe L'Erario

POPULAR WOODWORKING BOOKS
CINCINNATI, OHIO
www.popularwoodworking.com

read this important safety notice

To prevent accidents, keep safety in mind while you work. Use the safety guards installed on power equipment; they are for your protection. When working on power equipment, keep fingers away from saw blades, wear safety goggles to prevent injuries from flying wood chips and sawdust, wear headphones to protect your hearing, and consider installing a dust vacuum to reduce the amount of airborne sawdust in your woodshop. Don't wear loose clothing, such as neckties or shirts with loose sleeves, or jewelry, such as rings, necklaces or bracelets, when working on power equipment. Tie back long hair to prevent it from getting caught in your equipment. People who are sensitive to certain chemicals should check the chemical content of any product before using it. The authors and editors who compiled this book have tried to make the contents as accurate and correct as possible. Plans, illustrations, photographs and text have been carefully checked. All instructions, plans and projects should be carefully read, studied and understood before beginning construction. In some photos, power tool guards have been removed to more clearly show the operation being demonstrated. Always use all safety guards and attachments that come with your power tools. Due to the variability of local conditions, construction materials, skill levels, etc., neither the author nor Popular Woodworking Books assumes any responsibility for any accidents, injuries, damages or other losses incurred resulting from the material presented in this book. Prices listed for supplies and equipment were current at the time of publication and are subject to change. Glass shelving should have all edges polished and must be tempered. Untempered glass shelves may shatter and can cause serious bodily injury. Tempered shelves are very strong and if they break will just crumble, minimizing personal injury.

Distributed in Canada by Fraser Direct
100 Armstrong Avenue
Georgetown, Ontario L7G 5S4
Canada

Distributed in the U.K. and Europe by David & Charles
Brunel House
Newton Abbot
Devon TQ12 4PU
England
Tel: (+44) 1626 323200
Fax: (+44) 1626 323319
E-mail: mail@davidandcharles.co.uk

Distributed in Australia by Capricorn Link
P.O. Box 704
Windsor, NSW 2756
Australia

Visit our Web site at www.popularwoodworking.com for information on more resources for woodworkers.

Other fine Popular Woodworking Books are available from your local bookstore or direct from the publisher.

09 08 07 06 05   5 4 3 2 1

Library of Congress Cataloging-in-Publication Data

L'Erario, Joe.
    Creating the perfect wood finish with Joe L'Erario / Joe L'Erario – 1st ed.
        p.   cm.
    Includes index.
    ISBN 1-55870-744-1 (pbk: alk. paper)
    1. Wood finishing.   I. Title.
TT325.L45   2005
684'.084–dc22   2005001073

ACQUISITIONS EDITOR: Jim Stack
EDITOR: Amy Hattersley
DESIGNER: Brian Roeth
LAYOUT ARTIST: Kathy Gardner
PHOTOGRAPHER: Al Parrish
PRODUCTION COORDINATOR: Jennifer Wagner

Dedicated to my dad, mad scientist of paint, who died never having fully realized his dream to become a woodworker. I hope in some way I have fulfilled this wish of his and in doing so, have succeeded in helping you.

about the author

For ten years, Joe L'Erario was co-host of the television programs *Furniture on the Mend, Furniture to Go* and *Men in Toolbelts.* He has been finishing furniture since 1978, and has taught seminars on wood finishing and decorative finishes throughout North America. He is also co-author of *The Furniture Guys Book*. In addition, Joe is an artist who has been painting for as far back as he can remember. To view Joe's artwork you can log on to www.paintrunsdeep.com.

Joe has a son, Zane, from a previous marriage and spends his time in Philadelphia and Ottawa, Ontario, with his wife, Heidi, three stepdaughters, a smart cat and two really, really dumb ones.

acknowledgements

I'd like to thank Jim Stack and Al Parrish for their work on this project — especially for bearing the brutal Philadelphia heat wave over the week we shot the photos!

Thanks also to Danny Proulx for introducing me to Jim Stack.

Thanks to Mark Charry, owner and proprietor of Architectural Antiques Exchange (www.architecturalantiques.com) in Philadelphia, for allowing us the space to shoot the photos.

Thanks also to Jeff Brody, John, Dedrick, Dru, Bill, Greg and Pete, for their help and enthusiasm.

I especially want to thank my wonderful Heidi for her undying support, guidance and unending tolerance for my intolerance towards computers. Special thanks to my son Zane, Avalon, Avonlea and Paris, my brother Frank and his wife Ro, my pal and partner Ed Feldman, Art Miller for his guidance and all my family and friends in Philadelphia and Ottawa.

table of contents

introduction

When I was a kid, the odor of turpentine permeated my home whenever my father decided to paint the downstairs walls and trim, which, if memory serves me, was about every two years or so. This was in the early sixties, when latex paint was just filtering into the consumer market. My dad used oil paint, as all true house painters did, the same as his brothers did, as his father had, and as his father's father's father had. (He probably purchased it from Da Vinci way back in the old country!) Dad used oil paint because it was available and that's what he was familiar with.

Dad was also one of those people who simply liked the smell of turpentine. Naturally, with this kind of indoctrination so early on in life, it's no wonder my first marks in paint were performed using the variety of thickened paints I discovered at the bottom of old cans I'd found in the even older icebox under the cellar stairs. I was seven when I unearthed the treasures in that vault. I would pop the lids from cans, using the large screwdriver I'd often seen my father use (my top teeth biting at my lower lip as I pried). Then I would poke a stick through the hardened film to find an oily, viscous, amber resin bubbling

Where Do I Go From Here, 1983 marker and paint on wood 30" x 22" (76cm x 56cm)

through. I discovered that by stirring this resin vigorously, the paint would magically become the color it once had been.

This was my first notion of alchemy: that something clear, when mixed, could transform into a color. Whether brown, green or blue, the pigment I'd unearth at the bottom of the can with the turning of that stick would bring the paint back to life. The magic was in creating color from nothing, and anticipating which color it would be was the mystery I came to crave. I can still feel some of those paints saturating the bristles of some old brush as I'd pull and push them over the wooden legs of my dad's workbench. (I mention all of this as an introductory note because, besides refinishing furniture, I have painted pictures for most of my life. So, at any given time, the odor of turpentine is still present in my house in the way the aroma of fresh money wafts through the home of a Texas tycoon.)

People who have watched me on television and whom I have met at various trade shows always want to know if I went to school to learn what I know. I learned the art of wood finishing not at school but through trial and error over the past 25 years. The fact that I had started oil painting at an early age aided me greatly once I began working at wood finishing.

One of my major influences in the art of wood finishing, George Frank — a veritable pioneer in the wood finishing industry — graduated from the Academy of Wood Technology in Bucharest, so I suppose you could look that up in your spare time. (Just think: you could walk the land of the notorious 14th-century ruler, Vlad Tepes

Vlad the Impaler], or maybe visit Borgo Pass high in the Carpathian Mountains in search of Dracula's Castle.) If you prefer to stay closer to home, you could check out the local vocational schools that offer night courses in woodworking and wood finishing. Or you could just read books, like the one you are perusing right now! (See how I tied that all in?)

Wood finishing is not brain surgery. For the average woodworker, all you need to know is that it's all just stuff on a brush and common sense. You're going to need to know neither that silicon carbide sandpaper (used more in finishing than any other kind of sandpaper) is a chemical combination of carbon and silicon nor that it was invented in 1881 by Edward Abeson, who was trying to manufacture artificial diamonds. You also don't need to know that in water-based finishes, it's those doggoned glycol ethers (ethylene glycol monobutyl ether and propylene glycol monomethyl ether) that make alcohol and lacquer thinners compatible with water-soluble dyes. After all, this is celestial mechanics!

Back in the late seventies I worked in a cabinet shop where all they did was rub spar varnish into well-sanded wood. They never gave any thought to expanding the

finishing aspect of their business. In fact, they used one and only one recipe (which they swore by) even though they knew of others. They put it on floors, cabinets, bar tops, tables and doors. In short, they put it on anything they made out of wood. (Which, coincidentally, is what the company business card said in italics just below the company name: "…almost anything made of wood.")

By 1982 I was busy making cabinets as well as applying finishes to them. Then I landed a job at Architectural Antiques Exchange (www.architecturalantiques.com), a major source for architectural salvage on the East Coast. Their area of expertise was (and still is) the reconstruction and fabrication of antique bars, back bars and entire restaurant interiors. It was here that I began working with shellac, oil stains, aniline dyes, varnishes and lacquers while mastering the art of the old-world hand-rubbed finish. This knowledge I then brought to television audiences throughout the nineties.

So, right here at the outset (and you will hear it again before you close this book), I state that there is no perfect or ultimate finish. There are many possible finishes for a variety of projects that you'll learn about in this book.

Let's get started.

The Old Chair, 1991
oil and tempra on wood
29" x 12"
(74cm x 30cm)

1

uncovering the past

Many pieces of furniture purchased at flea markets, yard sales or even found in the trash can be restored with little effort as long as you are familiar with some of the techniques of the trade. For example, knowing which solvent works for which finish is half the battle won. You'd agree I'm sure, that breaking open a large smelling-salts-type capsule to revive a finish would be a perfect, effortless way to revive a finish, but until some company manufactures said capsules you will have to go about it the old fashioned way.

There are several types of wood finishes. Lacquer is the one that has been used most commonly by furniture manufacturers since 1900. It dries quickly, so many coats can be applied and rubbed out in rapid succession. Shellac was the preferred (if not the only) finish used by most furniture makers until about 1930. Varnish is another wood finish, but it is rarely used by furniture manufacturers because it dries so slowly. (See the sidebars on various finishes for more information.)

Before you can restore an old finish, you need to determine what kind of finish is on the wood already. The easiest way to accomplish this is to dampen a cloth with either denatured alcohol (methyl hydrate) or lacquer thinner. Lacquer will soften readily with only lacquer thinner or acetone (the main ingredient in nail polish remover). If neither of these solvents softens the finish, it is probably varnish. Some old varnish finishes are bombproof and will need to be removed with a paint and varnish stripper.

Once you know what finish you're working with, you can get started. To clean dirt and grease from old finishes, some books recommend washing wood surfaces with warm soapy water, but I say any water introduced into a finish is asking for trouble. Water on shellac? No way. The finish will turn white before your eyes, so don't do it!

The safest way to clean grime off a piece of old furniture is to scrub it with a soft brush and paint thinner (also known as mineral spirits or turpentine). Paint thinner and turpentine will not harm any finish. By

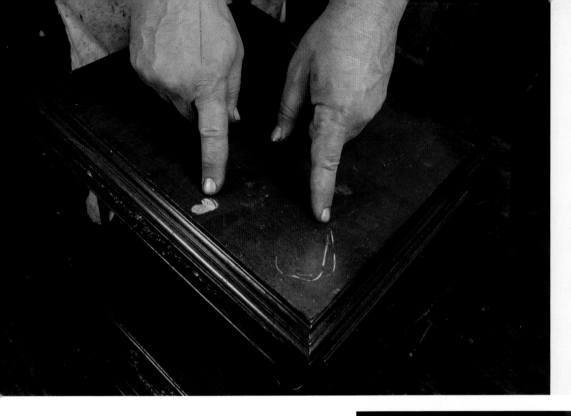

rubbing with a cloth (burlap dampened with solvent works especially well), you'll see the dirt and grime disappear from the wood. This remedy also serves to remove wax buildup. Be sure to go over the piece several times, using fresh solvent each time. If you've been trying for years to clean the sticky finish from the backs of your dining room chairs (especially in the humidity of summer), this is the technique to use.

Don't soak the piece; simply wet the cloth and rub, working on a bit of the furniture at a time. Once you've cleaned the area, wipe it dry with some soft paper towels and proceed to the next bit. Work from the top down. If the finish is in good condition, all you need to do after cleaning is to apply paste wax and buff the piece.

Here's a safety tip: Leave a bucket of water near your work area so you can immerse all solvent-soaked rags and paper towels.

cleaning and restoring old finishes

the shellac attack

When you've done a test with a bit of denatured alcohol on a piece of furniture or a length of wainscot and the shellac has softened or started to gum up, what do you do next? Easy. Clean the surfaces with paint thinner or mineral spirits, then sand the surfaces lightly with 320-grit silicon carbide paper. Sand evenly, with steady pressure. You don't have to go overboard by sanding all mouldings and carved detailing — unless, of course, you have a lot of free time.

Finish sanding, then dust all surfaces with a soft brush and tack cloth to remove any remaining particulate matter from the wood.

3

4

Go with the grain and don't load the brush so much that you cause severe drips. Drips will cut into the old shellac finish and will be very visible as drips. They may even dissolve the old finish, and then you will have to remove what you've just put on as well as the original finish. The trick is to be neat and graceful.

Straight from the can, most shellac is too thick to work with because it is made with a three-pound cut (meaning that three pounds of shellac flakes have been dissolved in one gallon of alcohol). Prepare a mixture of one part liquid shellac, (amber or clear) to four parts denatured alcohol. Brush this mixture over the entire surface. When I work with wainscot (shown above), I always begin with the raised panels, then work out to the rails (horizontals) and stiles (verticals). Do not go back and forth like you're painting the backyard fence with a wallpapering brush! Take your time and apply a nice, even coat.

5

Allow the finish to dry overnight, then rub it down with some no.0000 steel wool and paste wax. I always rub the same way I applied the finish; that is, panels first, then rails and stiles. Don't rub too hard or the friction created by the rubbing of the wool may soften the finish. Afterward, you can buff it with a clean, soft cloth.

This method is the quickest and easiest way to restore an old shellac finish.

6

facts about finishes

shellac

Shellac is the one naturally derived finish and has been around longer than any other type of clear coating. It is made from the excretions of the laccifer lacca insect, a parasite that enjoys mild-mannered meals imbibing the sap of the banyan trees of India. The excretions of these insects are deposited on the leaves and branches. When the branches are harvested, the excretions are separated, boiled, stretched, dried, broken up into flakes and bagged. *Lakh* is the Indian word for 100,000; hence it takes 100,000 insects to make one gallon of shellac. Shellac can be bought in flake or liquid form. It is a solvent-release finish, which means that once applied, its solvent (denatured alcohol) evaporates, leaving behind a glossy and durable film. Shellac has been in use from the early 1700s and was the only clear finish employed up until 1850. Ninety-five percent of all furniture found at flea markets, yard sales and auctions is finished with either shellac or lacquer.

lacquer

Lacquer is the finish most commonly used in the furniture industry today. Like shellac, it is a solvent-release finish. Its solvent is lacquer thinner. Lacquer's advantage is that many coats may be applied in a day. Lacquer is much more durable than shellac (which can be destroyed by a spilled cocktail while lacquer will not be affected). Because of its quick drying time, lacquer is usually applied by spraying. Therefore, it's an impractical finish for most home woodworkers. (Spraying is illegal in some areas and the noxious fumes can be a source of irritation to other neighbors, who might call the cops!) Brush lacquer is available and works well on small items like end tables, chairs, hall tables and small shelves. It cannot be used effectively on large surfaces because it dries too quickly.

varnish

Varnish is a reactive finish, which means that its chemical structure changes as the wet coating reacts with the air to become a dry, hard film. Because of its slow curing time, the furniture industry doesn't use varnish; but for the home woodworker, varnish is the way to go because it allows you to take your time applying it.

spar varnish

Spar, or marine, varnish is a great finish for outdoor furniture. After it cures, the finish remains pliable and able to expand and contract with the wood during temperature fluctuations.

polyurethane

Like varnish, polyurethane is also a reactive finish. Basically, polyurethane is liquid plastic, which is the major reason this finish is used on floors. It's also great for tabletops and bar tops. One drawback of polyurethane is that it cannot be rubbed out as easily as lacquer or varnish. At best, you can dull a gloss polyurethane to a flat look, but it will not have the same lustrous appearance as a rubbed lacquer or varnish finish.

paint

While paint is not recognized as a finish per se, it is a top coating and has been on the planet longer than any other stuff applied with a brush — except for marshmallow fluff. In its earliest forms, paints and decorative coatings were made from what people had around, like milk, berries and blood. Paint seals wood and that's the main reason for applying a coating to wood in the first place: to keep out moisture and prevent warping.

enamel

Enamel (and when I say enamel, I mean oil-based enamel) is gloss varnish with pigment. It's tough and durable but like oil varnishes, it needs time to set up. A dust-free environment (or as little dust as possible) is important.

oil and wax

While not finishes, oil (linseed, teak or Danish) and wax can be used to enhance the beauty of wood. If I've heard it once, I've heard it a million times about grandma's oil finish. Oil will look nice for a time, but eventually it soaks into the wood, making repeated applications a maddening necessity. Oil will collect dirt, feel sticky over time and won't give proper protection to the surface of the wood. Adding an application of wax is better than applying just oil; but remember, oils and waxes are not finishes. Wax is used to enhance tactile quality or, in the case of dark waxes, to hide scratches.

water-based clear coatings

While I am not an advocate of water-based finishes, they do have a place in the finisher's arsenal, especially in cases where allergies may be a problem or a nontoxic coating is required. Water-based finishes clean up with soap and water, dry fairly quickly and protect wood. What I don't favor is that they raise the grain of the wood and cannot be successfully rubbed out with steel wool or other abrasive techniques commonly used with oil-based and lacquer finishes. This, however doesn't mean they are not worth investigating. Experiment with them (as you should with all other finishes, too) so you will know where they might best be applied.

restoring a lacquer finish

Often, furniture that has been lacquered will become scratched or dull in some spots. There may be moisture blushes (as seen in this photo), the result of spilled water or wet glasses left on the surface. Recent moisture blushes can be worked out with a bit of lemon oil and cigarette or cigar ash; rub them in the direction of the grain with a soft cloth and then buff clean. The marks seen in this photo however, are old and stubborn but can be removed with a solvent. Lacquer is a solvent-release finish, which means it's possible to apply its solvent, namely, lacquer thinner, to areas of damage to restore the luster.

Mask off unaffected areas so they won't be damaged with drips of thinner.

Pour some lacquer thinner into a heavy plastic container, can or glass jar. (Thinner will soften or melt some plastics, so be careful. The last thing you want is to be holding the container over the surface when the plastic begins to melt, dripping thinner all over the place.) Apply the thinner in long strokes to the damaged area and let it sit.

Don't go back and forth over the surface as you would if you were painting. This will create nothing more than a mess because the thinner will soften the old finish and you will find yourself pushing around a mixture of thinner and old lacquer. Yikes!

Once the thinner dries (and it will dry quickly), take a look at what you have. You may need to apply succeeding coats to achieve good results, but make sure the previous coat has had time to dry. As you can see here, the lacquer has been softened enough for the trapped moisture to be released, hence the white marks are disappearing.

5

Remember not to brush with the usual back-and-forth motion. Once over lightly will do the trick.

6

Afterwards, this is how the top will look. The original lacquer as been reworked and has dried. Allow the piece to sit for 24 hours. Then, rub the top with no.0000 steel wool. If the finish looks good to you, finish rubbing using some paste wax with the steel wool. If the finish needs a little sprucing up, you can apply a light coat of aerosol lacquer. (Aerosol stains and lacquers are a reliable and essential part of the finisher's arsenal, although you are limited to touchups and small projects.) Apply the spray in long strokes, beginning two inches from the edge and ending two inches after the other edge. After it dries, rub the surface with no.0000 steel wool and paste wax.

7

padding out

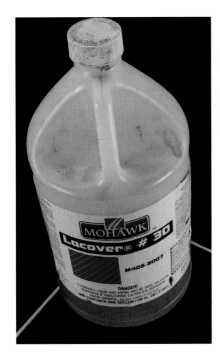

Padding lacquers are used to restore the even sheen and texture to a lacquered finish. Padding lacquers are acetone-based finishes that dry rapidly and are applied with a soft cloth you make into a pad.

1

Lay a square of cloth flat and fold the corners inward to the center. (Think diapers.)

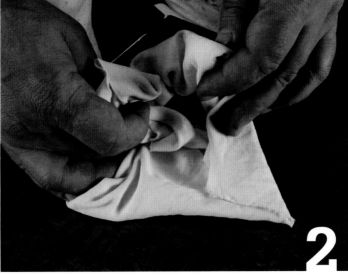

2

Now fold the corners inward again to create a diamond shape.

3

Gather the cloth together and twist it into a ball about the size of a large egg.

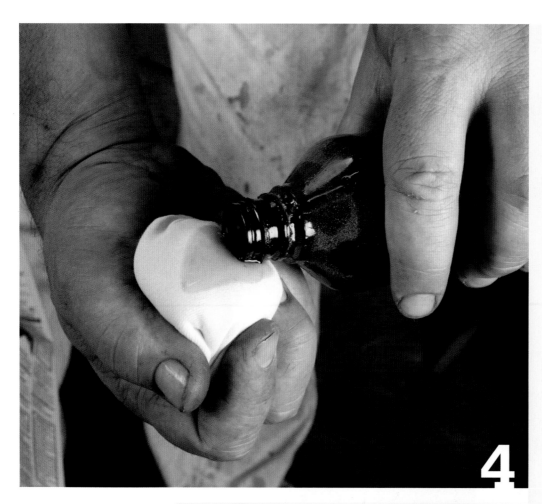

It's a good idea to pour some padding lacquer into a small bottle as shown here. This will make it easier to dispense than from a gallon container. Pour the padding lacquer on the pad and let it soak in.

4

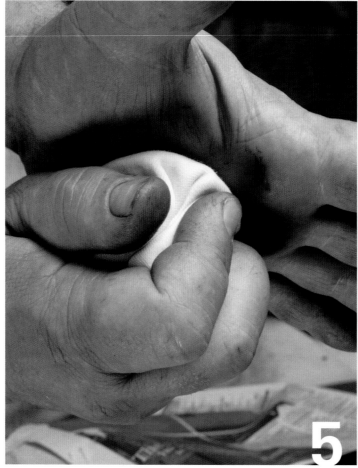

Tap the pad into your palm several times to disperse the padding lacquer evenly.

5

Start padding above the tabletop using a pendulum-type motion, beginning at one end and working your way across. You want the bottom of the pad to hit the surface on the downswing.

6

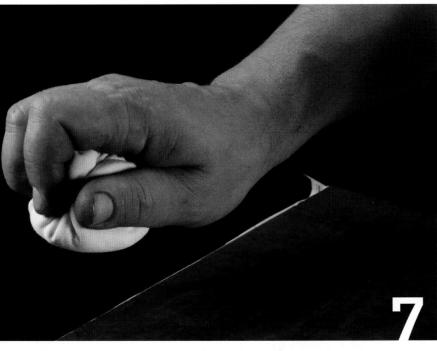

At the height of the arc — that is, once it has left the surface — you want to start the arcing motion backward, going back and forth, back and forth, back and so on, always with the bottom of the pad just barely hitting the surface of the wood. This is very important.

7

Repeat this pendulum motion as you move over the entire surface you are working on. Each time the pad hits, it will be depositing finish that will be plainly visible to you. It takes practice, but you'll be surprised at how easy it really is. Just remember not to stop midway to have a drink, leaving the pad and your hand stopped on the surface. The pad will stick, and you will be stuck refinishing the whole thing.

8

amalgamator

Amalgamators are usually a combination of methanol, esters, glycol ether and petroleum distillates. They can be used to soften and revive old finishes. However, as shown on this page, amalgamators don't work on badly alligatored finishes, because the finish has been destroyed by time and exposure to the elements.

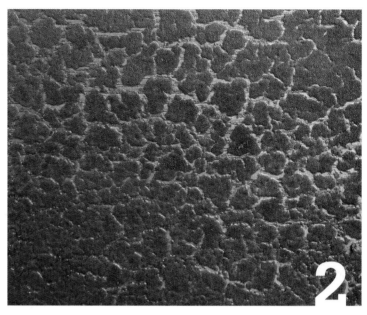

Badly alligatored finishes such as the one shown here just can't be helped. I don't care how many varieties of what are nonsensically referred to as amalgamators are on the market.

Amalgamators can be used quite successfully on thin cracking. However, with the kind of alligatoring pictured here you would have to rub for an inordinately long time to see any transformation in your lifetime.

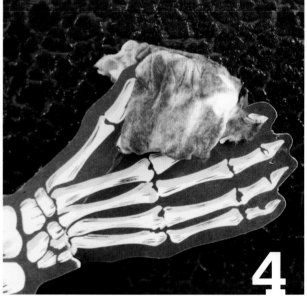

In fact, someone would have to remove your body and start where you left off, and then the sun would run out of fuel and everything would go dark and then what's the point? No one would be able to see the change anyway.

removing old finishes

By now I know what you're thinking: this reviving stuff is all well and good, but when do we get to stripping: the messiest, filthiest kind of work known to humankind? Right? Glad you asked. I mean it's messy.

Sure. Smelly? You bet — but then again, so is television these days, and yet people still watch! The important thing with stripping furniture is to have everything you need at hand, so let's take a look at these supplies.

clear-finish and paint stripping supplies

Left to right: no.0000 steel wool (lower left) for mahogany, pine and other soft woods, no.00 steel wool for denser woods such as oak, maple, walnut, ash, etc., wire brushes, a single-edge razor blade and an old-fashioned paint scraper (lower right) to get into corners.

Left to right: brass brush, gong brush, goggles, push-broom bottom, scrub brush, nylon-bristle scrub brush.

These are just a few of the finish removers available on the store shelves these days, along with some of the solvents necessary for stripping and cleaning wood. Lacquer thinner and denatured alcohol work best as cleaning solvents after the remover has bubbled your finish and you've scraped it off. Paint thinner, turpentine and naphtha serve well in the final cleaning stage. In the forefront of the group is lye, the old fashioned but still necessary product for some finishing work.

Top row, left to right: electric paint remover and heat gun. Bottom row, left to right at bottom: $\frac{3}{4}$"-inch chisel, various paint scrapers and a dentist's pick.

Here you see a bag of red cedar bedding, or "wood chips." Any kind of chip will do — except potato chips! (This bag is shown so you can see how readily available wood chips are, and also because the hamster's agent pressured me.) Wood chips such as those that come from a planer, jointer or router can help immensely with stripping, as you shall soon find out.

paper towels

I prefer to work with paper towels instead of rags because first and foremost, they are inexpensive and they are less likely than rags to snag on chipped wood edges.

Unlike rags, paper towels leave no lint residue when you apply a stain. (You usually don't notice the lint until you apply your clear finish. If this happens, the wood will seem hairy from the minuscule fibers of cloth that have stuck to the surface of the wood.)

stripping a clear finish

Here are three items we'll use to demonstrate stripping techniques: two pieces of moulding and a cabinet door. The beaded strip on the left is oak, the one on the right is a poplar egg-and-dart moulding and the door is a mahogany veneer with carved appliques. It's good to practice on small pieces first until you can get the hang of the chemicals and tools.

Now here's the first step. Shake your can. You don't know how long it's been on the shelf, so shake it a lot to get all the ingredients mixed up. Next, pour some remover into a small container. Now, instead of brushing the stuff on like paint (which is what most people do), try dribbling it on, dabbing it with the end of the brush as you move along. Remover works by creating a seal as it sets. This will ensure an even strip. Here I'm using an inexpensive disposable brush.

For mouldings such as this egg and dart, make sure the remover fills the grooves. Remember, some finishes are stubborn and some finishes just seem to melt away, but no matter what the finish, you still need to scrape and rub and wipe and poke and pick and rub and wipe again and again and again to make sure the wood is clean.

3

This picture demonstrates what to do with goop once it's scraped off. Just smear it onto a piece of newspaper and move on along. I like to use the front page and pick out the politician of choice for that day.

4

Once you've scraped off most of the goop, use paper towels to wipe off as much more as you can.

For beaded edges such as the one shown here, try to force your fingertips into the grooves to soak up the goop.

A typical clear finish (lacquer, varnish or polyurethane) will be ready to scrape after about 15-30 minutes. Use a flat scraper for flat surfaces only, not for carvings. You may also want to use some lacquer thinner and no.0000 steel wool. Use paper towels to absorb the extra moisture.

7

Puddles of remover left in and around carvings I deal with by using the wood chips I mentioned earlier. Wear gloves and don't forget to don protective goggles, because you do not want a single gooey chip flying into your unprotected eye. If you need a lot of chips, check the phone book to find the closest cabinetmaker and you can bother him for planer chips. He's just going to have to have them hauled away anyway. Right?

8

Whoa! I can hear you saying this while looking at the photo. What about all those chips stuck in there? It looks like a veal cutlet, for crying out loud!

This is where the gong brush comes in handy. These brushes are made of a same straw material as the street sweeper's broom (not that there is any longer a creature known as a street sweeper, mind you). By scrubbing the surface briskly with one of these brushes you will loosen any bits of old finish and/or stripper that have been trapped in the recesses of the carvings.

Take note: This is neither a simple nor an easy process. It can be a work-out because you have to work furiously. Be sure to wear goggles! Also, be aware of what's around you, because if some of the specks of remover-soaked wood fall on a finished surface they will scar it. So don't work in the dining room around your valued antiques.

11

Finish brushing with the gong brush. Use some de-natured alcohol and wash the piece down using an old-fashioned scrub brush. Once that dries, do a final wash with some naphtha, as I am doing in the picture.

12

Paraffin wax is the ingredient that makes most paste-type paint and varnish removers "pasty." Naphtha, paint thinner and turpentine dissolve wax, hence the final wash with any of these products.

13

Let the wood dry. Inspect the surface to see if there are any rogue patches of finish, which will appear darker than the wood. You will also be able to feel them. If you find some, apply more remover to the stubborn spots and proceed as above. Simple, eh? Now go get yourself a doughnut.

14

removing paint with heat

What you see in the picture is the prototype to the heat gun. It is called an electric paint remover (EPR), and boy do they ever work. I'm not even sure if they are on the market any longer, but you may be able to find one at a flea market or the common junk store. I bought two of them back in the mid eighties and they're both still in working order. You can see the heat of the filament in this picture; it heats up to about 900°. EPRs are used in conjunction with various scrapers, and will aid greatly in removing several layers of paint from the wood. They can also make toast if you are working through lunch.

This pediment from a 1920s-era wardrobe facade is perfect for demonstration. The idea is to hold the EPR on the surface. The contact area is about 4" x 7" so you can burn off a section this big at a time. As you develop more skill in handling an EPR, you will be able to move in a straight line and peel off wide sections of paint at a time. "Why not just chemically strip?", you may ask. Good question. I've always preferred this method for heavy paint removal because it saves on remover. By stripping most of the paint off with an EPR, you will spend less on remover and solvent and save yourself a great deal of time.

Here, you can see how a curved scraper fits nicely against a rounded moulding.

3

The same scraper's straight edge works equally well against a flat edge. These scrapers are available at most paint stores and home centers. It is called, naturally, a moulding scraper.

4

When using an EPR, you must pay close attention to not burn the wood or, allow the paint to ignite. If this happens, blow it out quickly. EPRs are not recommended for stripping off old clear finishes, as they will ignite rather rapidly. Work outside and be sure to wear a mask with filters suitable for lead paint fumes, as old woodwork and furniture may be coated with lead-based paint. If you are doing something that is attached to the wall — say, old wainscot — make sure you have some fans blowing and the windows open.

5

Here the moulding scraper's pointed edge removes paint from a quadruple bead. (Well, I'm removing the paint — the scraper's just helping.) But you have to be careful when applying a metal point like this to wood, because there is the chance that the point will get away from you and scar the wood on a diagonal.

6

Here you can already see the beauty of the aged walnut, partially revealed, that was underneath all that old paint. Some stubborn stuff still remains in the star carvings and other crevices of the rope moulding.

This is the time when you bring in the chemical remover. I'm using some orange remover. The nice thing about this remover (Citristrip) is that it stays wet for 24 hours, so you can easily apply the stuff and let it sit overnight. Also, if you want to, you can use a heat gun and some sharpened pieces of stick to dig out the gunk as it softens, and then go on with the chemical remover.

For small items such as this crown moulding, it's a good idea to pour your solvent into a tray of some sort. The one I'm using is an old industrial steel pan that I found in the trash. (Yes, I still trash pick!) The white handled brush that looks like an iron is a nylon-bristle scrub brush, which I'm using to keep the surface of the wood wet.

Notice that I am wearing rubber gloves, a must for this kind of work. Do not use surgical gloves when working with solvents — especially lacquer thinner. They are much too thin.

Even after all that burning, chemical remover application and washing with solvent, you will still have stubborn spots: there's just no way around it. This is why it makes me laugh when I see infomercials on television heralding the arrival new removers that are supposedly so "safe" and "easy" and "amazing" that they work in only one application — and you can even do it in formal wear! Believe me, if that were true, I'd be showing you how to do this while wearing an opera tux.

11

But in reality, as you can see, it's back to applying more chemical remover.

12

using peelable paint remover

Peelable removers are caustic, meaning they are usually lye based. With caustic compounds, there is the possibility of the wood discoloring, especially oak or walnut. However, this kind of discoloration can easily be eradicated by using common household bleach once you've removed all the paint. You must wear gloves and goggles when using peel-away removers.

Peelable removers are thick, almost the consistency of joint compound. They are applied with a scraper (shown) or with a plastic trowel that sometimes is attached to the bucket. Because the peelable remover is so thick, there is no fear of it falling off the surface it's been applied to. For baseboard mouldings (should you have it in mind to renovate your house or apartment complex) peelable removers can save great amounts of time and aggravation. Just trowel it on. Sometimes, the product may come with a roll of special paper that you press onto the applied remover. After 24 hours, just pull off the paper and the remover and old paint will follow.

Once the peelable remover has been applied, you need only wait for the old paint to soften. Go ahead and read a Jackie Collins novel.

As you can see, after only a short while, the first few layers of paint have wrinkled and may be easily scraped away.

I wasn't at all patient and began scraping before I should have (only because I wanted to get on to the next section of the book). In many instances you will have to reapply more remover because you never know just how stubborn your paint is until you start working with it. Some old paints out there can be as durable as battle armor.

I reapplied the remover and went through the process once again. More satisfying results are plainly visible here. Oh, by the way, I never did do the other side of the pediment.

2

smooth and easy does it

Most people make their worst mistakes in the sanding process. That's why I'm a staunch advocate of spending more time cleaning the old wood, once you've removed the goop with repeated washings of solvent in lieu of sanding. Naturally, there are times when you have to sand, as in the case of burns and watermarks, for example. Most of the time, however, it's wiser not to sand, as you will see in upcoming pages.

I have seen some absolute horror jobs in my day. I remember the beautiful 35-foot mahogany bar-top that had been sanded with a huge floor drum sander, the rampant hills and valleys caused by the rolling steel drum visible only after the varnish had been applied. Then there was the dining-table top whose beautiful crotch-mahogany veneer had been completely sanded off by the unwitting amateur refinisher, armed with a machine as deadly as a weapon of mass destruction. And why? The family was coming for Thanksgiving dinner; and naturally, sanding was the fastest way to make the table presentable. Ha!

I'll never forget the hapless woman who once brought a cabinet door to my shop wanting to know what kind of wood it was because of the funny smell she had detected while sanding with her trusty quarter-sheet palm sander.

"You sanded through the Mylar facing!" I said, looking at the flakeboard underneath.

"Well...is it good wood?" she wanted to know.

Yikes!

sanding

For sanding wood, there are only three types of sandpaper you should bother with: aluminum oxide, garnet and silicon carbide. The higher the number of the paper, the finer the grit. Shown above are various grits from as low as 40 (far left) up to 220 (far right). The lighter colored papers are aluminum oxide; the orange paper is garnet, the paper most preferred in the woodworking trade.

Finishing paper is used for sanding between coats of finish as well as rubbing out the final cured top-coat finish. It can be used dry or in conjunction with lubricants such as water or paint thinner for a "wet rub." Finishing paper grits start at 220 and continue upward to 700 and 800 grits. For your jet-liner you can even find grits exceeding 3500!

Machines such as the half-sheet orbital sander and belt sander are useful additions to your arsenal when resurfacing is necessary. Cigarette burns, old and dried black water rings from wet vases and glasses can sometimes be impossible to remove without heavier machinery than the arm, unless you are Popeye. (Did you know that before he got into cartoons he was a wood finisher whose specialty was the famous French polish?)

Before using power sanders, it's important to understand when it's appropriate to use them and when it's not. In the hands of an inexperienced woodworker, a belt sander run over a veneered top will surely cause damage. And the orbital should always be followed up with hand sanding in the direction of the grain to remove any squiggle marks left behind by the orbital action of the machine's pad.

The mighty power of a belt sander is able to remove old finish quicker than vying television networks can create another reality show. It is very important to keep the machine flat and steady at all times without exerting more pressure toward the front or back of the machine lest the rotating drum-wheels leave their prints on the wood.

1

The only disadvantage of removing finish with a belt sander is that old finish will soften under the heat of friction and the belt will gum up quickly. So if you are prepared to sand away your finish, I would suggest you keep a lot of belts on hand.

2

Balance is the most important thing to remember when using a belt sander. You must move with the machine and keep it steady while exerting a controlled amount of downward pressure on the surface you are sanding. Notice the cord of the sander placed over my shoulder. This helps greatly when you are moving alongside a long stretch of wood. With the cord over your shoulder you are less likely to run over it — something I have done more than once in my time. First time was right out of the womb. I ran over my umbilical cord with a toy truck.

Allow yourself plenty of room to sand the surface in one continuous motion.

It's important to remove sanding dust so you can see what you are doing. Even dust collection bags will not gather all the dust, so give yourself the brush.

5

Here the clean, almost new-looking mahogany is very apparent next to the old finish. Once you've removed the old finish, you can sand with the orbital sander. Then, finish up by hand sanding in the direction of the grain of the wood to remove any machine-sanding scratches.

6

A full sheet of sandpaper is best folded three times. Whether a full sheet or half sheet, fold it thrice. You got that? Nice.

7

Most people tear their paper into irregular scraps, ripping it up as if they were tearing romaine for a salad. How are you supposed to work with this kind of stuff?

8

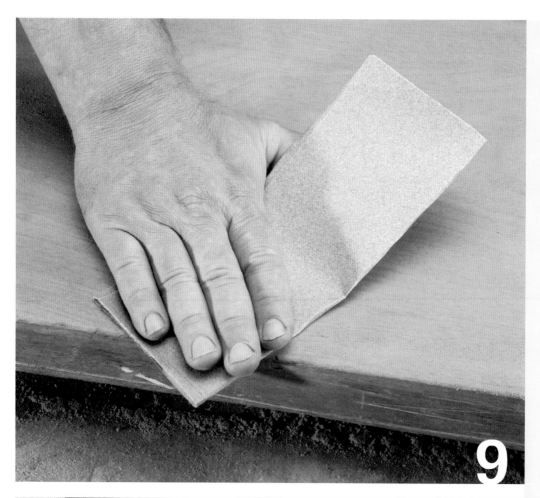

With the fingers placed on top of the paper and the thumb underneath, your paper will work so much better for you. Turn the paper as needed once it becomes clogged. You can then fold and unfold until all areas of the paper have been used.

9

Wetting the wood with water, once it's been sanded, will not only show you the true beauty of the wood, it will also raise the grain.

10

After the water dries, hand sand with a finer grit of paper and cut those raised grain fibers off. This will result in a much smoother surface.

This technique of wetting the wood after sanding is extremely useful if you are planning a natural finish such as a straight varnish, lacquer or polyurethane coating, or as preparation for an oil and wax finish on birch or maple. By the time you have finished wetting and sanding with finer grits of sandpaper the wood will feel absolutely smooth and will be ready to topcoat with clear finish. Wetting and sanding the wood in this way will also greatly reduce the amount of grain-raising under any water-based finish. This seems to be a major problem for many of the people I have spoken to in the past who have used WBF's. Remember: no matter what the label may claim, *any* water-based finish is going to raise the grain of the wood.

sanding swirls

Sanding swirls are the bane of my existence. No matter where I am, if there's newly finished wood before me, I find myself inspecting for swirls. They're a telltale sign of sloppiness and inexperience.

Understand the concept here: wood is soft. An orbital sander — if it's a decent one — is heavy, and people have a tendency to bear down too hard. Once you pull the trigger, the pad is going around 360°. Then the machine is being dragged back and forth across the surface by the operator like someone spreading fudge! Inevitably, the paper will clog, and the clogs (buildups of sanding debris) are going to leave impressions.

Once you've made squiggle marks they have to be sanded out by hand; there's no other way around it. You can see from the picture how etched they are into the wood. If these are not sanded out the next problem arrives once you apply a stain. Squiggle marks appear more evident and unsightly because they soak in more stain and appear darker. In the end, the dark squiggle marks will be magnified and quite apparent under any clear topcoating because clear finishes magnify imperfections in wood.

sanding through veneer

Whereas plywood veneers can measure up to $\frac{1}{16}$" thick, some flakeboards can be covered with veneers that are as light as $\frac{1}{32}$" thick. So you can imagine how running a machine over these may cause irreparable damage. Think of it as dermabrasion for the veneer.

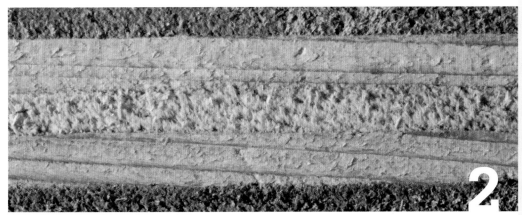

This is the magnified edge of plywood and not a cross section of delicious layer cake.

Now here's a magnified edge of flakeboard — or is it a shot of my Rice Krispies treat?

Cabinet-grade plywoods can be covered in veneers that are about $\frac{1}{16}$" thick and should never be sanded with too coarse sandpaper.

cleaning versus sanding an old finish

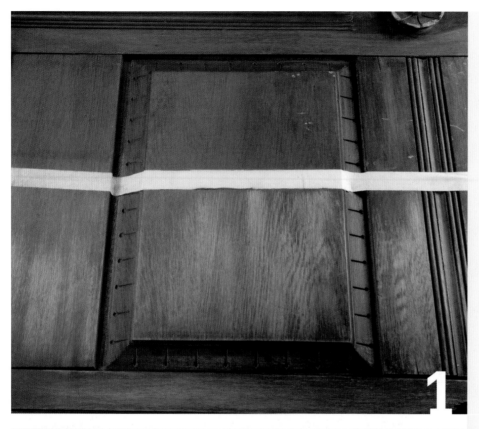

The photo shows the difference between cleaning an old finish (above the tape) and sanding it (below the tape).

One reason for not sanding old wood is because sandpaper will break into the *patina*, or, the color the wood has attained over many years. It's not advisable to "spot-sand" either. Let me explain. Suppose there's a dark mark in the center of the panel and it's bugging you to no end. What do you do? You will do what most would do and that is to wrap sandpaper around a finger and begin sanding away in an effort to make it go away. But all you succeed in doing is creating a light spot that's going to show through any applied stain. Once sandpaper has broken the surface, the entire are *must* be sanded.

Here, after having cleaned the upper portion of the panel with a bit of paint thinner and steel wool, I'm applying a new oil stain.

I applied the same stain to the portion of the panel where I sanded off the finish too.

Wiping away the stain from the cleaned section leaves an evenly coated surface.

On the sanded section, however, you can see where the old finish remains at the edges of the center panel.

When this happens, it is possible to actually sand stain into the wood.

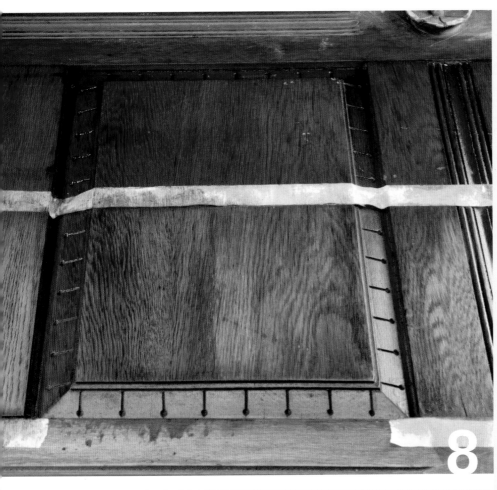

The action of the paper cutting into the wood will allow the stain to enter and create a much more even finish.

When the stain dried, both sections of the paneled door were coated with amber shellac (what used to be called "orange"). On the top is the section I cleaned with paint thinner, stained and then recoated with new shellac. The bottom section serves to demonstrate what happens when sandpaper is taken to a finish that doesn't need to be sanded. Once you begin, you must sand the entire surface to attain an even look. And while the bottom half may look "cleaner" I prefer the top effect because the old look has been preserved.

3

the wonderful world of color

The wood finisher's arsenal will include not only the typical products used for regular finishes, but also some items that may be used to create "special effects" (although none of these involve having to deal with George Lucas's Industrial Light and Magic!). Resourceful wood finishers have been using common household products to get uncommon results for years and years, with great success.

You might have heard people refer to furniture with a bleached look as having a "pickled" finish. The term may not be 100-percent accurate, because a true pickled finish is created by applying a paste of un-slaked lime and water to the wood, and then breaking off the lime after it hardens; but "pickled" is often used to describe any finish where the natural pigmentation of the wood has been removed. There are a number of common products that can be used to achieve this effect.

Another popular "special effect" is the weathered or aged look. Rather than wait for a century or so, you can get that antique appearance right away by using lye. Lye can destroy wood, burn the skin and singe the nose hairs, as well as dissolve the bristles of a brush. But when carefully used, the results are near to perfect for creating weathered appearances. Other artful effects can be created by coloring the wood with dye, stain and paint, as you shall soon see. So, turn the page and divine some secrets of finishing prestidigitation!

the lacquer finish

These are the most common items used for bleaching the color from wood. Oxalic acid is a weak bleach and is usually mixed with water. The sanding dust from wood treated with oxalic acid can irritate nasal passages, so be careful. Laundry (chlorine) bleach is next on the list. Also shown is a two-part hydrogen peroxide bleach.

A collection of plywood and solid-wood boards that have been bleached are shown at left.

The wood at the far left is mahogany; the other is oak. The small blocks in front have both been bleached using laundry bleach.

When using the hydrogen peroxide bleach (or any chemicals), be sure to wear gloves and goggles and use a disposable brush. The *A* solution is applied first. This caustic agent cleans the wood.

Wood Bleach
Use on wood only when mixed with Solution B.
A SOLUTION
Blanqueador de Madera

Here I'm the applying *A* solution to a piece of mahogany.

Once the *A* solution has been applied, apply the *B* solution with a clean brush.

A foaming action takes place as the bleach starts to work. Leaving the wood in the sun while the bleach is working will increase the desired effect.

using lye on wood

Lye can be used to age wood before your very eyes. Its chemical name is sodium hydroxide and it comes in the form of small crystals. Lye can cause burns so take care when using it. If you're trying to match a piece of new wood to an old one, a little bit of lye mixed in hot water will allow you to color the new wood more effectively than an oil stain. Lye may be used as an under-color before you apply an oil stain.

You can see here how the wood washed with lye gives a new piece of oak the yellow color of aged wood.

Once the lye has done its work, it is necessary to neutralize it with an acid. Plain white vinegar works well.

3

The wood can now be lightly sanded and finished. To make this sample look even older, I could apply some amber shellac — say, two to three coats — rubbing with no.0000 steel wool after each application dries. Then I could wax the surface using plain old black shoe polish. Forcing the polish into the pores of the wood would result in a look reminiscent of mission-style furniture.

4

As you can see, lye applied to cherry instantly gives it that aged look — like my aunt Mickey who spent many of her years basking in the sun.

I once used this technique on a 4' x 8' sheet of cherry plywood used to replace a water-damaged panel in a conference room. The builder had replaced the panel and tried to mimic the color of the other panels using a store-bought oil stain. The other panels around the room had been installed years before and had only been varnished; Mother Nature had done the rest. Cherry darkens over time, so I sped up that time using the correct proportion of lye crystals to water. Next, I neutralized with vinegar, sanded lightly with 320 silicone carbide paper and then finished with several lacquer coatings. Once installed, you couldn't tell the new panel from the old ones. Compare the old cherry drawer shown at left to the new cherry piece washed with lye.

using ammonia on wood

I mentioned mission-style furniture earlier. This style was invented by Gustave Stickley back in the early 1900s. Many said that Stickley's simple furniture was cumbersome and too plain, but it was functional. What it also had going for it was that the wood was oak — a lot of it quarter-sawn (or as it's called by those who are unfamiliar with that term, "tiger oak," because of the radiant grain lines that are visible when the wood is sawn this way). Before Stickley finished his furniture, he had the wood fumed in large canvas tents. The fuming agent was 100% pure ammonia. By comparison, today's all-purpose cleaning ammonias are only 10% to 20% ammonia. Given time to react with the tannin in the wood, the gas would render it a warm brown color. After the wood was treated this way, it was shellacked many times and finished off with an application of black wax that, through rubbing, became trapped in the pores.

What you see here is not as exotic as Stickley's process, however, regular household ammonia brushed directly onto oak and some mahogany will render a definite change in color.

adding colored wood filler to wood grain

After sanding this bleached piece of oak, I pulled a wire brush across the wood to remove any dust trapped in the pores. Remember, oak's pores are deep compared to maple's. Be sure to wire-brush with the grain and not across or perpendicular to it. Wire brushed *will* scratch badly.

Once it was dusted, I coated the wood with a mixture of one part clear shellac to five parts denatured alcohol.

Using some standard plaster (found in any home improvement center) I mixed a paste of plaster and added some dry pigment to color it.

The mixture should have the consistency of smooth peanut butter. Rub it into the wood with your fingers, going around and around in little circles, forcing it into the pores of the wood.

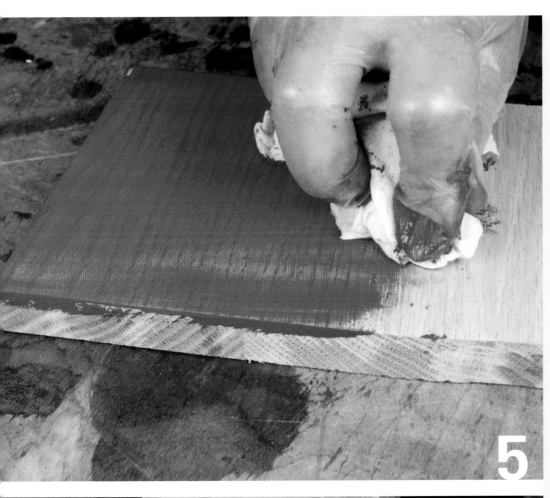

Rubbing across the grain with a cloth removes the excess. Don't rub with the grain at first because you do not want to pull the filler from the pores. Going across the grain will prevent this.

5

Finish off by lightly rubbing parallel to the grain.

6

Ahh. A group shot. The filler and the filled. You can see how the pores stand out and say, "Now, look at me, people!"

Once the filled wood dries, finish can be applied over it. Make sure to remove every trace of excess filler before you apply your top coat; otherwise the final result will be as unsightly as those nasty squiggle marks we saw a few pages back.

7

8

Using paint instead of the plaster mix will create much the same effect on open grained wood like oak. This photo shows a panel of French oak filled with white paint.

coloring wood with black shellac

+

= black shellac

Black shellac cannot be bought; however, to match certain dark finishes it can be produced by using old 78rpm records. In the early 1900s through to the late 1940s, 78s were shellac-based. Breaking a record to pieces, placing the pieces in a jar and then covering them with equal parts of denatured alcohol and lacquer thinner will dissolve them (after 24 hours) into a black liquid which is, no foolin' — black shellac!

After 24 hours, I can just barely hear the receding harmonious sounds of Guy Lombardo...

Strain the undissolved record parts from black liquid shellac.

3

I once matched some interior church mouldings that had been replaced by the same guy who had replaced the cherry paneling. Having not learned his lesson from the last time, he once again tried going the way of the oil stain, to no avail. I cleaned off as much of the oil stain he had applied using lacquer thinner and steel wool. When dry, I sanded the wood lightly and washed the wood with my lye solution. After I had neutralized, I wiped the wood down with some paper towels and when thoroughly dry, applied some artist's burnt umber oil color (available by the tube from an art supply store). In the picture I'm using a burnt umber Japan Color. The left two-thirds of the wood in this photo was first washed with lye and then neutralized. The right third is the wood's original color.

4

After the oil color dried, I applied a coat of the strained black shellac to the wood. I could tell with the first application of this material that I was on the road to completion. A second coat, rubbed out and waxed once it dried was the ticket.

5

If you place your hand over everything in this picture but the balustrade and the piece of oak, you can see that the color is unmistakably matched. And in the church where I performed this magic, any difference is even less noticeable because the area where the mouldings are located is dark.

Now a top coating such as this is not the ideal type of finish for an entire piece of furniture, and I am not advocating such an application. However, in the event that you should have to match mouldings in a church or some similar detailing in your own home, you'll know what to do with those old 78 records.

6

using tinted polyurethane

Nowadays, people want to get things done fast, so manufacturers of finishing products have obliged by formulating top coats that have coloring agents added to them. These coloring agents are nothing more than specially formulated stains. Oil-based varnishes as well as polyurethanes can now be purchased with pigment. This is an effort to halve the time you have to spend on your laborious project, but believe me, any attempt to achieve a good finish in half the time is only asking — no, begging — for trouble.

It's not that these tinted products do not work. They can and do. However, it is best to stain the wood first before applying them. In this photo, the left side of the wood has been coated with tinted polyurethane on raw wood. You can see brush marks; that is, lines of heavier poly/stain, which is the runoff from the edges of the foam brush.

I'm using a synthetic bristle to apply tinted polyurethane to the right side of the wood, which was stained first. Applying the polyurethane with a bristle brush instead of a foam applicator lessens the possibility of getting bubbles in the finish.

Here and below you can plainly see the difference that prestaining makes.

The reason the grain is so much more visible on the right side is that the original stain accentuated the pattern; that is, it entered the grain and allowed it to become more visible. On the left, the pigmented polyurethane is lying directly on the bare wood, hiding the grain in much the same way as would paint.

4

the big finish

In this chapter we will look at many wood finishing products currently on the market. While I can't spend time describing much more than the major characteristics of each product, you will certainly learn enough to decide which products to purchase. Whether you're starting with bare wood or with a piece that has been stripped, there are some basic steps you need to follow in order to achieve a nice finish.

Keep in mind that it is not necessary for you to understand the scientific properties of every paint, stain and varnish; the important thing is to remember what is compatible with what. Naturally, oil products and water products will not and *cannot* work together. Likewise, oil products will not be compatible with alcohol products.

The information in this book will help you choose products that will give you the best possible results for any wood finishing project. You should also realize that items such as grain filler, aniline dyes, padding lacquers, aerosol lacquer tone sprays and quality brushes can only be purchased from woodworking supply houses.

Home centers and paint stores carry the basic manufactured oil stains, varnishes and polyurethanes, as well as common solvents, but you'd be hard pressed to find quality varnish brushes. And when you're finishing, you have to know when a throw-away brush will work just as well as a $40 brush and when that $40 brush is going to serve you better than that throw-away. Just to give you an example, I do a lot of work on bar-tops, either finishing newly constructed bars or stripping and coating bar-tops after-hours in restaurants. Each top usually receives three coats of quality bar-top varnish, and, while I may apply the first two coats using a $7 "all paints" brush, the final coat is always laid on using a $125 badger-hair "flowing" brush. A brush like this is perfect for applying a smooth coat because these will leave little or no visible brush marks in the dry varnish. Also, with a brush like this, I know I'm not going to have to worry about finding any rogue hairs stuck in the dry film.

Deciding on which products to use may seem like an intimidating task, but it really only involves a bit of knowledge, and hey, you've already got your nose in the right pages.

So get going already!

sealers and clearcoats

Shown here are a variety of stains and coloring agents for changing the color of wood. Paint can be thinned and applied in washes (thin layers) and sealed between coats of shellac. Japan colors are oil pigments ground in oil and mixed with japan driers. They are able to be mixed with paint thinner or turpentine to form their own stains as well. Popular oil stains come already mixed and ready to apply, while ultra-penetrating stains and aniline dyes can be mixed with methanol for deep, penetrating effects.

Shown at far left is shellac in both colors: *Amber*, or what used to be called "orange" and *clear*, or what used to be called "white." Clear shellac is the bleached form of amber and is used when you want a completely clear coating. Amber shellac applied over, say, a white pickled finish, will turn it a mustard color. The polyurethanes, polyshades and varnishes also shown work well on all types of interior wood, while spar varnish (far right) is the preferred finish for items to be used outdoors.

Shellac is by far my favorite finish, and really, the more you work with and learn about it, the more you realize how versatile it is. Shellac is used both as a sealer and as a top coat. It can be purchased in dry flake form (usually in 5-lb. bags) or in liquid form (in cans). As I already explained, the liquid form is usually too thick to use straight from the can and must be further diluted with denatured alcohol. Did you know (of course you probably don't — that's why I'm telling you) that in the old days, if you had your hat "blocked", (and I'm not taking about your baseball cap either, but the feathered fedora or drum-like derby) it would have been repeatedly sprayed with shellac in order to form and harden the felt. Even more fascinating, as you found out in earlier pages, they used to make records from it. I'm sure you'll agree that on this information alone you have invested wisely in this book!

Like most things, brushes come in many types. What would it be like if you could buy only one type of brush? As it is, there is a brush for every need, from the tiniest single-haired sable to the widest varnish brush. On the far left is a rounded staining brush. In the center, is a "flogging" brush used for decorative painted effects. To its right, is my favorite $125 badger-hair varnish brush. Top right are some common bristle brushes and bottom right are some disposable foam brushes. Never use foam brushes for shellac or lacquer because the foam will dissolve.

Wood fillers are necessary for nail holes, dings and certain dents. Most come already mixed, but some (such as Durham's, shown) need to be mixed with water to reach the desired consistency.

Grain fillers are available in neutral and various wood colors. These are usually thinned with naphtha or mineral spirits to the desired consistency and applied to the wood across the grain. They fill the pores of the wood so that succeeding top coats may render a mirror-like finish.

This photo shows four different stains on a piece of maple. Maple is one of the most difficult woods to stain because of its density. From left to right: a commercial oil stain, an aniline powder dye (which has to be mixed with methanol and water), a gel stain and a methanol-based ultra-penetrating stain (UPS). Though similar to the aniline powder, UPS comes already mixed and ready to use. The best choice for staining maple, as evidenced by the sample pictured, is certainly the aniline powder stain. With these and the UPSs, you must wear gloves or you and your furniture will look like relatives: These products stain flesh as well as they do wood.

For touch-ups, thin brushes and dry pigments mixed with varnishes, shellacs or lacquers are used to repair and color scratches and other minor surface flaws. I like to save coffee can lids to mix my pigments and clear sprays in. Pigmented aerosol lacquers (seen at right) can be purchased in many wood colors. These are pigmented lacquer sprays used best to tint and evenly shade areas that have already been stained.

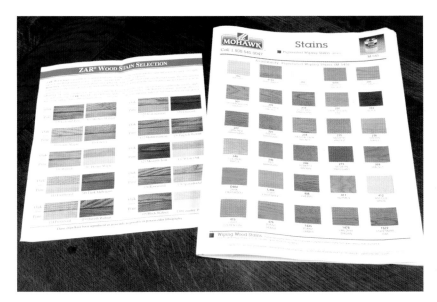

Wood stains come in many colors. Every company seems to have its own name for each stain: what one may call "Golden Oak," another may call "Harvest Oak."

Japan colors are available in a variety of hues and can be mixed with varnishes and lacquers for various effects. They also may be added to commercial oil stains for heightened tonal qualities.

clear finishes

This photo shows one piece of oak with three types of clear coating. On the left is a gloss furniture varnish. The middle jar contains what is referred to as "crystal" soya-alkyd-resin varnish, and on the right is a water-clear lacquer. Each lends its own color to the finished wood.

Fisheye flowout is an additive developed to combat silicone contamination. Silicones from easy spray-on-wipe-off polishes contaminate the wood but are never noticeable until you strip something and begin to recoat it with a new finish. Silicones, clogged in the pores, will prevent the varnish or lacquer from "flowing out" evenly and will appear pockmarked. I use fisheye flowout in all the varnish and lacquer I apply to stripped furniture. Eight to ten drops per quart does the trick.

grain filling

Grain filler is much too thick to use as it comes from the can. (You can also see how this stuff can easily be mistaken for fudge icing.)

Scoop out the amount you will need, then add a bit of naphtha to thin.

Mix the filler well until it has the consistency of mayonnaise, not Miracle Whip — yech!

Before using the grain filler, seal the wood with a spit coat of shellac: one part shellac to five parts denatured alcohol and allow to dry.

Once the shellac has dried, sand the wood with 320-grit silicon carbide paper. Wipe dust and blow all traces of particulate matter from the surface. Apply the thinned filler across the grain perpendicular, as shown.

5

You can also rub the filler with burlap using a circular motion. This has always been my preferred method of application. In this way you are applying and removing some of the excess at the same time.

6

Give the filler half an hour or so to set up and then remove the excess with some fresh burlap and brisk rubbing. First rub across the grain...

7

...and finally with the grain. Allow the wood to dry overnight; then you may proceed with the top coat of your choice. If you stained the wood with a UPS or aniline dye, however, do not — repeat, DO NOT brush shellac or lacquer over the surface because either of these finishes will re-constitute the dye on the wood and smear.

8

touching up

touch-up markers

Furniture touch-up markers can be bought separately or in a handy assortment roll. Every color you could possibly need — and some you'll never even use — is here in what I like to call my "Lee Van Cleef ammo-roll-sling." These are available from mail-order finishing supply houses.

Touch-up markers are part solvent, part drier and part pigment. Applied properly, they can hide a surface scratch in an instant — just don't expect to hide a major surface injury on your Italian gloss-lacquered dining room tabletop. Use a doily and a bowl of lemons instead.

wax sticks

Wax sticks are another means of hiding the types of scratches that expose the raw wood, such as those from a cat's claw or a minor split or crack. Wax sticks will become soft when held in the hand because linseed oil is usually added to the wax in the manufacturing process to make them malleable.

The idea is to select the proper color and rub it across the crack with enough pressure to force it into the split.

...or a few different ones in an effort to mimic the background pattern of the wood itself.

Once the wax has been applied and forced in, an old credit card can be used to scrape away the excess.

Once the excess has been scraped away polish the area, with a soft cloth. After it hardens you can go over it with touch-up markers or some dry pigment mixed with lacquer (discussed on the next page). Remember that wax is not for massive holes but only for minor cracks. Finishing supply houses also offer what are called "low-heat sticks" in the trade. These look exactly like wax sticks, but they must be heated with a hot knife over the damaged area until the melted liquid drips into the wound. The excess can then be trimmed with either a razor blade or a plastic card.

burn-in sticks

The third and most difficult method of fill is called a "burn-in." Burn-in sticks are made from shellac and pigment that have been heated together and poured into molds. Each stick is about the size of a pack of PEZ. (Boy, am I showing my age here!) Shellac sticks come in a variety of colors, and, like low-heat sticks, are heated with a hot knife or soldering iron until the liquid drips into the damaged area. Once filled, the excess is sanded away using solvents and felt pads. Repairs range from very successful on, say, the side of a piece dark walnut or mahogany furniture, to "iffy" on a tabletop — especially one with a glossy white or black lacquer finish.

painting with dry pigments

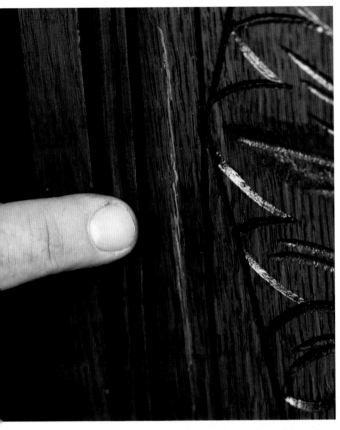

Scratches on the edges or sides of furniture (such as those made by cats) can also be hidden — in many cases more effectively than with markers — by actually painting a color over the scratch.

Using a fine bristle brush, mix some dry pigment with shellac or spray lacquer. The color of old oak can be successfully matched using burnt umber, burnt sienna and yellow ochre.

Apply the paint with a steady hand, using more sienna or more umber where needed. Remember, oak has a definite grain, so you'll need to mimic light and dark spots to make the damage invisible. Allow the paint to dry for an hour or so; it will dry flat. Then go over the repair with some straight shellac or lacquer. If the line of repair is glossier than the surrounding area after it dries, you can break the sheen with a light rub using #0000 steel wool.

rubbing and polishing a finish

"Rubbing out" a finish is not something that is done much these days. In fact, you may find on certain labels of cans of clear finish, the notice: *gives that hand-rubbed look* — but just what does this mean? And how can it give "that look" without having been hand rubbed? Most people seem to think a finish doesn't have to be rubbed out, or that rubbing out is an unnecessary step — three coats of lacquer or varnish on the wood and that's that. But I say, if you've already gone that far (especially on a top surface) why wouldn't you want the finish to feel as good as it might look? One thing to remember if you are considering rubbing out a piece is you should always use gloss lacquer or varnish. Satin and semi-gloss finishes contain flattening agents (talc) which produce low luster results. When a satin surface is "rubbed out" it will feel smoother but will not render as much of mirror finish as gloss coating will.

To rub out a final coat of finish start by wet sanding with the grain using 320 silicon carbide paper. Either plain or soapy water may be used. This step will eliminate any dust that may have settled and become trapped during drying time. Rub evenly across the surface, using steady pressure. Be careful of edges where you might break through and expose the wood under the stain and finish. When the paper starts sticking to the wood through suction, you will need to change paper. You can wrap sandpaper around a felt block to wet sand if you like, or just use your hand on the paper. The white on my fingertips is the abraded finish combined with residue from the silicon carbide paper.

After wet sanding, clean the surface of all gray powdery residue with water and paper towels. For the next step, I use #0000 steel wool. For small areas, a pad the size of a shredded wheat biscuit can be torn into three equal-sized pieces and rolled in the hands to make smaller pads, as shown.

3

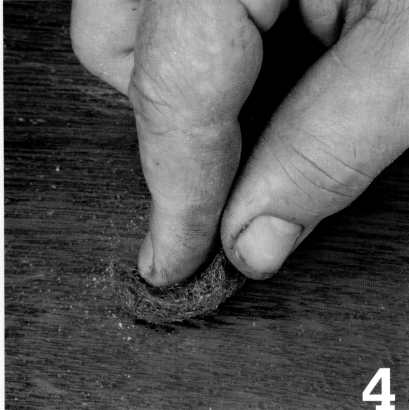

Small pads are good for doing the edges and any rubbing on carvings or mouldings. Like sandpaper, steel wool clogs and needs to be discarded when you feel it's not "cutting" any longer. Save those bits though; you can always use them for stripping.

4

Larger rolls of steel wool for rubbing out top surfaces can be made by unfolding two or three pads and sandwiching them together.

5

From one end, begin tightly rolling the unfolded pads together. I usually use two unfolded pads with a regular pad as the core.

6

Now that's a pad! This will serve you well. You can see traces of dust on the bottom of the pad. As this layer builds, the pad will stop "cutting" — that is, doing what it's supposed to be doing, namely, polishing the dried film of finish. Once you get the hang of it, you will be able to feel exactly when it's time to unfold the pad and then roll it tightly again, exposing new areas of clean wool.

Keep an even pressure on the wool as you rub. Be particularly cautious with shellac, as the heat generated by the friction of rubbing can actually soften the shellac and damage the finish.

If you have a lot of free time on your hands and you want to go that next step after the steel wool, you can use pumice and rottenstone with water. Pumice (on the block of wood on the left) is powdered volcanic ash and comes in grits from 1F to 4F with 1F being the coarsest. Rottenstone is decomposed lime stone, gray in color and seen on the block of wood on the right These may be used with water or mineral oil to further abrade the finish. I learned to do this step with these traditional powdered abrasives, but by today's standards they are outmoded. Car polishing compounds offer the same effect with much less aggravation. After this rubout, waxing is in order.

9

After using a polishing compound, I apply a coat of Butcher "amber" wax or Minwax dark wax, depending on the color of the wood.

10

Finally, polish the surface with a soft cloth. If you've done a good job, you should be able to see yourself. Tell yourself, "Thanks." It make take a while for you to master the art of rubbing out a finish, but the reward will be great, especially when you place a beer on the table and see its reflection — but don't forget to use a coaster, you animal!

restoring an antique desk

In this project, I'll demonstrate how to restore the finish of an actual piece of furniture, using techniques described in the section on cleaning versus sanding an old finish in chapter two. No sanding will take place.

The problem many people subject themselves to once they've acquired a piece of furniture is trying to decide what they want to do with it. The piece of furniture you see at right certainly could have been stripped and refinished but it's never made sense to me when people choose this solution. Never has. I suppose there are people who see the collecting of furniture as an eclectic and glorious remembrance of the past, of a time when things were made to last and prefer to leave their treasures the way they found them. Others will imagine how their new acquisition is going to fit into their color scheme, or to change the wood, or to paint or pickle, or to make the dark wood lighter, or vice versa. As you might have guessed, I belong to that first group!

The restoration of this Belgian oak writing desk took three hours of labor with very little effort. I used no strippers, machines or spray finishes. (I did, however, sweat considerably.) I began the transformation by cleaning the entire piece with paint thinner. Paint thinner, as I mentioned earlier, will not harm any finish. A 1-inch sash paintbrush enabled me to get thinner into the corners. I next wiped away all residue with some paper towels and left everything to dry.

Shellac was the way to go next. I mixed up a sealer coat of one part amber shellac to four parts denatured alcohol and brushed this mixture over the entire surface, working from the top down.

1

Be careful not to overload the brush with shellac or it will drip all over the place when you are going over edge mouldings.

2

Knowing in what order to apply a finish is second nature to me, but others may be intimidated, standing there with a brush in one hand and a container of finish in the other, unable to decide where to start. What you need is a game plan. I started at the top, moving around the top edges, the "apron", and then down every leg before finally applying shellac to the brace system that holds the four legs together.

Sanding came next on the list of things to do. I know I said,"No sanding will take place," but what I meant was no machine or production paper sanding with garnet or aluminum oxide — the kinds of papers that are used for sanding raw wood before finishing. These papers would certainly break through the finish. What I used was a 320-grit silicon carbide paper to lightly sand the new shellac I had applied.

4

After basic dusting, I used a tack cloth to remove all remaining particles. Made of cheesecloth impregnated with neoprene, tack cloths are great for removing all traces of sanding dust.

5

After breaking the tack cloth out of its wrap, peel it apart. Don't use it flat; it's meant to be opened up and used the way you see me using it. You need only apply gentle pressure, too. The tack cloth will do the rest.

6

Keep turning the cloth, folding it in and around it self to allow it to eat the dust, so to speak. Once the dust sticks to the cloth you can't shake it free. Keep one of these in a jar with a lid and it will last forever — but hey, they only cost a buck.

7

Because tops of tables, bureaus, sideboards and desks suffer more wear and tear than their frames, the only part of this project I coated with varnish was the top.

8

I'm using an alkyd (oil-based) furniture-grade gloss varnish, pulling and moving the varnish over the top and then going from side to side, parallel with the grain to get rid of any drips.

9

Use a dry brush around edges; that is, do not dip it into your container to pick up more finish because you will have the runoff from having gone from side to side to move around. I also run my finger under the edge to wipe away any varnish that may have had the chance to form into a drip.

10

Because I did not want the top to have a more finished look than the rest of the desk, I allowed the varnish to sit for half an hour or so, then proceeded to rub as much of the varnish off as possible using a piece of balled-up burlap. After allowing this to dry overnight, I gave the top a good rubbing the next morning with no.0000 steel wool and applied a dark paste wax for the finishing touch. Still has its age-old charm, wouldn't you say?

11

2

creating a weathered bench

You know what I love about this kind of project? You can do it, then hand it down to your kids and tell them it's a bona-fide antique! With any luck, they'll never know the truth until you finally spill the beans or you die; even then, they may still swear it's original!

Working on unfinished furniture is a great way to learn about finishing materials and how they act on unfinished wood. At the unfinished furniture store you can find pieces made from oak, pine, maple, sometimes walnut, sometimes cherry. One thing is for sure: You certainly won't have to worry about repairing anything, as you would with an old piece of furniture you found in the trash or purchased at a flea market or yard sale. Moreover, there's no stripping involved: just the new wood, you, and whatever products you've chosen to

effect the proper finish.

Along with many different types of wood furniture, you can be sure that the unfinished furniture store will also have its own line of stains and top coatings that they will try to sell you at premium prices — offering as much insight on how to apply the stuff as you yourself can glean by reading the instructions on the back of the can, for cryin' out loud.

No matter. You can purchase products from them, or you can visit the home center of your choice to gather what you need. You can do a natural finish, or you can apply a stain and then a top coat of varnish, lacquer or polyurethane. Or, you may want to try something a bit more fun, a bit more stress-relieving and in many ways, a job that's really hard to screw up! So, what are you waiting for? Go find a subject. I'll wait.

What I was looking for at the unfinished furniture store was something newly made, preferable oak, that could actually be made to look old without appearing contrived. Let's face it, what they call "distressing" nowadays is little more than a craft activity — especially if you take into account any of the recipes presented on television make-over shows. Certainly, the crackle medium would be the reigning king of distressed finishes. True. Anyone can do it, right? All you have to do is follow the instructions on the can, right? I can always tell this kind of "distressing" from the real thing, however, because usually no one goes the added distance to first make the wood look old and worn before applying the finish coat.

Even with the liquid "crackle mediums" available almost everywhere these days, it's impossible to make the surfaces of something that may have been constructed this year look like the thrilling days of yesteryear by simply adding a magic painting medium. No, to create an effective fake one must go the added distance. That's why I'm going to physically beat this wood into shape by subjecting it to violence because, well, I was born in South Philadelphia.

Any weapons you have on hand will do: chains, rocks, hunks of wood (that's a 2" x 24" hunk of bubinga next to my left hand), ice picks, submergence in the local pond, buckshot, Tonka toys — even the grating sound of Rod Stewart destroying Cole Porter has been known to be effective.

Always wear safety goggles when doing work like this. You don't want stuff flying into your eyes. Keep in mind also, the all-important "war face" which is crucial for convincing the wood. At this stage in the game I have organized my attack plan. The assault in yet to come.

It looks like I'm having a brilliant idea here (but maybe it's just indigestion from the shrimp salad I ate the night before). An old bench could have two planks for a top instead of one, I told myself. Why not? And the line created by the two planks would certainly make for a more interesting design.

3

Running the single plank top through the table saw at the midpoint did the trick, giving me two identical planks. For production-line purposes, this bench was made from six pieces of wood. It cost 80 bucks after the store's markup, so the bench probably cost the factory 40 bucks to make. If another step — like cutting the top in half — had been added to the mass-production process, well, that would take more time, and more time translates into more money out of your pocket when you go to purchase. So if you want a convincing fake, you have to add your own features.

4

5

One of the most universal design shapes is the diamond. As a raised panel, an applied panel or a more rustic form cut-out, you can find this shape on many different styles of furniture through the ages. Using a combination square's 45° edge, I merely drew lines to form a diamond on each end of the bench.

6

Using a drill and a ¼-inch bit, I drilled holes inside the diamond. You can see, I had to place the diamond closer to the top than to the center to avoid running into the cross brace that runs from end to end.

7

A jig saw is the only way to go here. I used a scroll-cutting blade and followed my pencil marks around to each drilled hole until the piece fell out.

8

I cleaned up the diamond with files and sandpaper just to get rid of the rough edges and any splintering — which, on a job such as this, can only add to the charm of the piece. I'm going with the imagined idea here that some old cooper (a barrel maker) threw this bench together in his spare time.

Now we're ready to begin the distressing assault. In this photo, I have already taken a bastard file to the edge of one of the top planks. I'm fitting it on the bench to get an idea of how it's going to look. On the floor is a ten-pound bash hammer, good for denting sharp, new corners.

9

Chains work well on top surfaces, but you must use them carefully. Yes, even when distressing, care must be taken so that you don't make all your marks with the chain running in the same direction. That would look contrived.

10

Using a bastard file, or rasp, cut all of those hard edges away. You may want to wear work gloves when using one of these because they have the tendency to shred flesh. Don't be afraid to let go. The only way you can fail is if all your marks look too contrived. Just think worn and weathered — like the difference between a new Ralph Lauren trench coat and Columbo's.

11

Continuing, I ran the bastard file down the outside and inside edge of both ends, using the flat of the file as well as the file's sharp edge like an axe.

12

Turning the bench on its side allowed me to scrape away the smooth, well-manufactured arch of the bench ends, too.

13

I don't know if this picture was taken before the mighty strike, on the pull back, or after the strike. Whatever, it made a pretty good dent.

14

Here, I am working on one of the top planks with the bastard file. I definitely have a vision while I am going along. As with sculpting, it has to feel and look right.

Running the length of the top plank with the file. I remember that the weather that day was particularly grueling: 98° or 99° with 100 percent humidity. Here's where I seemed to spring a leak. The sweat came pouring from the brow, dripping from the tip of the nose...yes, I like to think of the wood and me now, as one.

If you are working on a project like this where pieces can be disassembled and worked on separately, make sure you turn them over and on edge to, well, literally "work them over" the way I'm doing with these top planks.

Finally, I have a chance to sit down while I work! Shoeshine, anyone?

18

In real time, I think I may have worked for a couple of hours trying to make the bench smooth and worn-looking. Sitting, standing and kneeling. What fun. What exhilaration! What a pain in my knees!

19

No longer in possession of a fingerprint, I continued filing. I remembered my uncle Vito. He had removed all his fingerprints with lye. He was a safe-cracker.

20

I scattered an assortment of brick pieces, crushed stones and rocks on the floor of my workshop, then stood the bench on end on top of it. Standing lightly on the back end, I literally ground the wood into the rubble. Take that!

A quick call to the quarry on my "Bedrock" cell phone.

Once I had completed the dirty work with my chains, mallets, files and rocks (I didn't have any Rod Steward so I settled for Paul Anka), it was time for a soothing drink. One Alaskan-Polar-Bear-Heater later and it was time for sanding.

After being brutalized, all edges and surface areas should be sanded. So, using some 80-grit aluminum oxide paper, I feathered all the rough edges, easing any gouges, chips and wounds.

Naturally, while sanding you will come across areas that may need a bit more attention. Aarrgh! Ahh, that's better.

25

Now, to add some color. In the annals of staining, no concoction is more fascinating than this stuff which looks like a swamp and smells like wet, rusty metal — because that's what it's made from! I've had more people ask me about this coloring agent than any other and so, rather than describing it earlier when I talked about other types of stains, I thought I'd feature this old "swamp cooler" in its very own project. For the bench, I mixed equal parts of white vinegar and water and threw in all the rusty iron I could find. If you want, you can wet some steel wool and leave it out to rust and then use this in the liquid. Let it sit for a few days or up to a week and it will begin to foam and look, well, pretty much like your average, run-of-the-mill, polluted swamp or lake — or, in this day and age, the ocean of your choice.

26

Next, strain the liquid through a fine paint strainer (available at paint stores or home centers).

27

This solution works by interacting with the tannic acid present in the wood. Oak contains more tannin (tanic acid) than other woods so the darkening effect is heightened. Pine and poplar contain little tannin, so this mixture will do nothing for them but turn the wood a sickly gray-green color. Some mahoganies may go black, as will some cuts of walnut — and certainly your bananas if left out too long. The effect is also dependent on how strong your concentrate has become which, in turn depends on just how much rusty iron you've used. Be sure to test your solution before applying it to your project. The first application on this piece of scrap oak shows the instantaneous change the concoction can cause.

After only a minute I was able to determine that the wood was going too dark (to black), so I chose to dilute the concentrate by adding a little more water.

This picture gives you an idea of the varied intensities of stain this concoction can make. As you can see, the first brush mark I made (bottom of picture) has gone to black. Above, in succession, are three more watered-down patches. The patch I am pointing to is what I was looking for. When dry, this dilution of the liquid concentrate will render a satisfying grey color on oak, much the same as a weathered stockade face.

Applying the "swamp cooler" is no more difficult than applying a common stain. Pay close attention, however, to what's around you. Whatever is nearby that isn't finished — woodwise, that is — will become stained if splashed. Use a cheap, throw-away brush. I recommend wearing surgical or rubber gloves since the liquid may stain flesh. One time I labored a few hours working with this stuff doing a matching job where I needed to tone the new wood to the worn color of the striped old wood. I was so eager to get started I neglected to don my surgical gloves and afterwards I had to use straight bleach and a pumice stone to clean them.

There's always a spot that's missed, but it's easily found, thanks to the stark contrast of light to dark wood. All you need do is dab a bit of solution on the light spot.

Do a final wipe-down of the top. You can see how evident the grain is as the wood begins to dry.

Here's a full shot of the bench after I applied the vinegar and rust solution.

34

35

36

You will know when the wood is dry. Wet patches are pretty clearly discernable to the eye because the wood has a flat, worn look. If you apply water or anything water-based, i.e., latex paint, water-based stains, water-based polyurethane or the vinegar/rust solution, the grain will rise.

I mentioned this earlier and I will reiterate: No matter what the label claims, any water-based product will raise the grain. If the clean-up instructions on the back of the can say water cleanup, you can expect the grain to rise. After the wood is dry you will feel that it is quite rough. I sanded the bench using 220-grit garnet paper, being careful not to exert too much pressure because I didn't want to break through the black color and expose the white wood beneath. After sanding, I dusted off.

Here we are back to shellac. After mixing up a wash coat (you should know this by now: one part 3lb shellac to 5 parts denatured alcohol), I applied the mixture to the wood using my trusty 2" badger-fitch brush.

37

Working quickly, I scrubbed and covered all areas readily visible as well as those underneath. The top planks were coated on both sides as well as all edges. This is one of the major aspects of finishing that people fail to understand. Even with something as simple as this bench, you should coat all surface areas with finish, such as shellac, so that the wood is protected from moisture which can seep into the wood. MOISTURE=WARPING=HEADACHES. If wood starts to warp, you can bet that moisture has gotten into it and caused it to swell and curl.

38

After the shellac dried, I sanded the wood using 320-grit silicon carbide paper to make the surface smooth again. You must always sand between coats of finish in order to build up a smooth final finish. No ifs, ands or buts!

39

Yes, that thing in my hand is a wire brush. This is going to sound crazy to you but don't worry, I'll bet I've done this a million times on a million different pieces of oak furniture (well, OK, maybe hundreds).

40

I'm pulling this wire brush down the length of the wood in order to clear out the pores so more of the stain I will be applying will be absorbed. I have smaller wire brushes for edges and the like.

41

I used a Minwax special walnut stain as the vehicle (base) into which I mixed a bit of yellow ochre japan color. Japan colors will thicken a stain to produce a kind of paint, which is what I wanted.

42

Here I am adding some burnt sienna Japan color to the mixture.

43

Notice I am wearing my surgical gloves while applying my oil color. If there's one thing experience has taught me, it's that *too* much time can be spent cleaning one's hands at the end of the day. Gloves will prevent aniline, chemicals and UPS's from dying your flesh and while stains are much more easily removed from flesh, it's the cuticles and under the nails you will have to labor over with a grimace. A box of gloves costs ten bucks and is worth it.

44

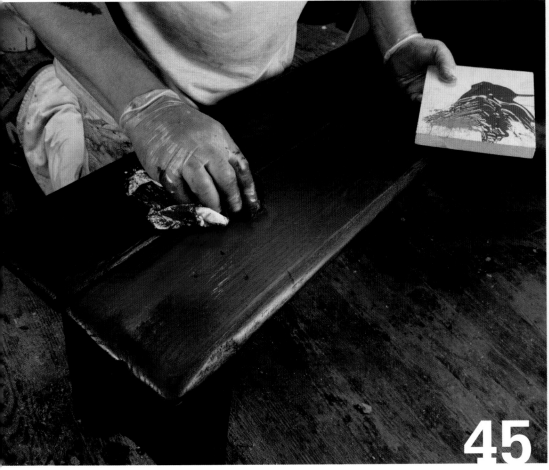

I always use paper towels to remove the excess, and also to dab a little more color in spots that might need additional pigment. The block of wood in my hand has some of the colors straight out of the can on it, both sienna and ocher.

45

Wipe off the excess evenly — especially when your other hand has been resting where it shouldn't be! Hey! Who took my sandwich?

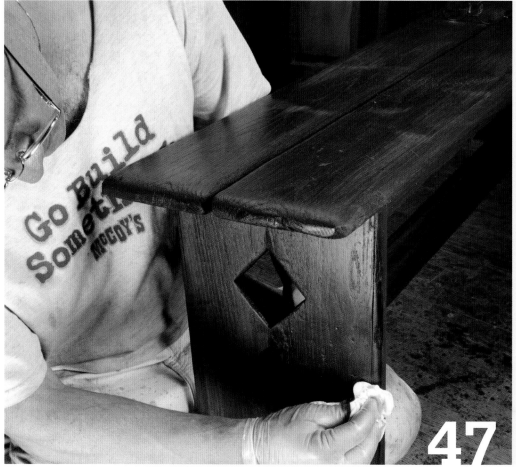

Here I am comforting the bench just like I saw Dr. Phil do when I was over to his house for dinner. Remember anytime an oil stain begins to dry out on you, a bit of paint thinner on a rag or paper towel will easily allow it to be moved around and evened out.

Ahh, an artful shot, don't you think: the wiper and the wiped. Some would say — and many who have looked over my shoulder while I have been working have — "Well, if you put a stain that thick and dark on, why'd you have to go and put that swamp stuff on first?" Well, that's an honest question, so I'll give you an honest answer. If I hadn't applied the "swamp cooler" to the wood, the bench would appear much lighter in color. Anyone who's every tried to paint a white wall green knows it will take four or five coats of green before you achieve a uniform color. The same applies to wood stains. In the long run, having the darker "vinegar and rust" color will render a much more even, overall tone.

48

I would have had to apply three or four coats of stain, sandwiched between succeeding wash coats of shellac to achieve what I did with one coat of oil stain and one washcoat of shellac. So here's a lesson for you: To save time and reduce steps, use the swamp cooler.

I allowed the bench to dry for a couple of days and then shellacked it once again using a wash coat with the same proportion of shellac to alcohol (1:5). When the shellac had dried, I sanded lightly using worn 320-grit silicon carbide paper, then I wiped off the dust with a tack cloth.

The application of a coat of varnish gave the bench the look you see in the picture at the beginning of this project. My total labor time (not including drying time, of course) was probably no more than three hours. The outlay for material was about $50.00.

The bench now sits in my apartment in Philadelphia and serves as a table from which I enjoy pizza and a beverage while watching anything but reality shows on television. I have yet to cause a white ring or moisture blush!

Happy distressing!

49

questions and answers

Q I have kitchen cabinets made of pine with birch fronts. They are 35 years old and were varnished. I want to refinish them. I was told by an acquaintance that I could not do this because the wood has absorbed the varnish, so a refinishing job would not turn out properly. It also has been suggested to me to just paint over the cabinets. I really don't object to having white cabinets; however, I would rather have them natural or stained with a clear finish. I want them to look new and not tacky. Can you please help me?

A First of all, don't listen to what people say — especially if they don't know what they are talking about. There's nothing in life as annoying as the know-it-all master-of-all-things who goes around giving advice, remedies and solutions to problems he has only heard or read about, but never attempted himself. Your cabinets can be stripped. For someone to tell you that the wood has absorbed the varnish and therefore can't be stripped is ludicrous.

Birch is a dense wood with tight pore structure that ensures easy stripping. Moreover, even if the finish is 35 years old, it will come off magically with the right stripper. Use a solvent-based stripper. If the back of the can says to rinse with water, do not use.

I would pop all the doors and lay them on a flat surface: sawhorses with a sheet of plywood always works. If you are going to attempt to do the doors in place, extinguish all pilot lights because strippers are highly flammable. (See chapter one for stripping details.)

After all surfaces have been stripped and cleaned repeatedly with fresh solvent, do a final wash-down with paint thinner and allow everything to dry overnight. You can then apply a varnish, polyurethane or lacquer finish.

If you decide to paint the cabinets, clean all the wood surfaces, sand the wood with 220-grit garnet sandpaper, dust and wipe them clean with paint thinner and then apply a good oil-based primer. When the primer dries, sand lightly with 220-grit aluminum oxide sandpaper, dust, wipe with a tack cloth and apply your paint. After the first coat of paint dries, sand with 320-grit silicon carbide sandpaper, dust with a tack cloth and apply the second coat.

Nothing to it.

Q Years ago I spilled some perfume on my cherry-wood dresser and night table as well. The varnish got gooey and bubbled off. (It was Halston's perfume for women — go figure.) I went to the store where I bought the furniture and asked how to fix the problem. They sent out a guy who used a marker to color the blemish and then sprayed some kind of spray on it. Needless to say, it looks crappy and I'd like to know how to get it to look better. Do I have to strip the top and revarnish?

A If ever there was a common problem, it's perfume spilled on a dresser or night table. Most perfumes are alcohol based, which is damaging to most lacquer finishes. (Ninety-eight percent of all commercial finishes today are lacquer.) This makes perfume the number-one pain in the you-know-what.

Actually, the only way to fix a badly scarred top is to refinish it. The process for stripping is the same as described in the previous answer. The only problem you may have is matching the color. Since you didn't mention which color of cherry the finish is (and there are many variations of the "cherry finish") I can't help you there.

By the way, the guy who came to fix (or hide, shall we say) your particular problem was probably on contract with the store; he simply attempted to cover up the defect as quickly as possible. However, no blemish such as this can be eradicated or fixed merely by using a marker and clear spray. While markers are good for inconspicuous areas, they won't hide scars like those created by spilled perfume on a lacquered surface. A large vase would work better!

Q We have a wonderful dining room table. Unfortunately it has some dings in it from being moved many times. Also, there are white patches caused by placing hot canning jars on it. We want to refinish it, but my father-in-law said it had some kind of coating on it that we would not be able to strip. Have you ever heard of such a thing? If so, can we strip? If we can't strip it, can we at least repair the white patches?

A Does your father-in-law know the guy who told the other people they couldn't strip their kitchen cabinets? The only things that can't be stripped are baked-on epoxy coatings, and I hardly believe that your table has one of these. It doesn't sound like you've tested any kind of remover and have relied solely on your father-in-law's powers of deductive reasoning. So, I suggest you do a test to find out if the top can be stripped. To do this, apply a bit of remover and see if any bubbling occurs. If so, proceed with the process.

The white patches are caused by moisture trapped beneath the finish. This is the same as the white ring that can be created on an unprotected finished surface if a wet glass is left to sit overnight. Sometimes white patches can be removed with a lubricant such as lemon oil and some cigarette or cigar ash rubbed in the direction of the grain. However, this works mostly on freshly made marks. More stubborn spots can sometimes be removed with fumes from a ball of cotton soaked with clear ammonia. Simply hold it over the affected area so the ammonia gas can pull the moisture from the blush. But the best method to remove the marks is to apply a padding lacquer. (See the section on padding lacquers in chapter one.)

If the stains have been there for years and you don't want to try any of the above, a vase of flowers will serve as well; maybe with a nice, festive doily beneath?

Q I built a country cupboard for our bathroom from knotty pine, and I want to put a pickle finish on it. There are some blue accents in the bathroom and my wife wants to know if the pickle could be tinted a slight blue using a stain. If so, please tell me how this could be done and what to use.

A Yes, by all means this can be done. If you are using oil pickling, add some blue oil color or some blue oil paint that best matches your accents. How much blue to use is your call. Once you are satisfied with the color, thin the paint using paint thinner until you reach the consistency of an oil stain. Then brush it on. Wipe it off after half an hour, leaving some of the blue pickling in cracks, crevices and mouldings. Be aware that the yellow of the pine may show through. In combination with the blue pickling stain this may cause it to appear green. My suggestion would be to

pickle using white. Then, any mouldings and detail work can be painted a blue to match your blue bathroom accents.

Q How do I make a black wax for my mission furniture?

A Black wax can be made using beeswax and black oil pigment or black dry pigment. Buy some beeswax and shave it down with a chisel until you have slivers (kind of like grating cheese). You may be able to find some tiny balls of beeswax for sale in bags at an art supply store. Place the shavings or balls in a glass jar and cover them with paint thinner or turpentine. Overnight, the solvent will melt the wax. Mix some black oil color or black dry pigment into this melted wax and stir. Now you have black wax. Or, you can save yourself the trouble and apply black shoe polish.

Q I have three or four good brushes I came across while cleaning my garage that are rock hard because I neglected to clean them. One is a nylon-bristle brush and the others are Chinese bristle brushes. Is there anything I can do to make them right or should I just throw them out?

A Give the nylon brush a decent burial. It's gone. It's dead. If paint or varnish was used with the other brushes, they can be brought back to life by immersing the bristles up to the ferrule (the metal band that holds the bristles in place) in lacquer thinner and letting them sit for a couple of days. You may want to change the lacquer thinner and let them soak a little more. Wipe the bristles clean and dry. You can even use a wire brush to scrape the bristles if the paint is stubborn and then soak some more. If the bristles are hard because of latex paint, bury them alongside the nylon brush. Then go get yourself some new brushes.

Q Every time I varnish I always end up with bubbles in the dry finish. What am I doing wrong?

A This is another common problem. There are a few reasons why bubbles occur. If you've shaken the can instead of stirring, if water gets into the varnish, if your brushing action is too fast or if you scrape the bristles against the rim of the can, bubbles can be created. If you do get bubbles, let the finish dry. You can then sand these bubbles away and carefully apply the next coating.

When applying varnish with a brush, instead of scraping the brush on the rim of the can as you would with paint, dip the bristles into the varnish and then tap the inner side of the can to allow some of the varnish to drip off the bristles. After tapping, put the brush onto the surface you're going to varnish, pull back and then drag the brush forward. Continue this dip-and-drip, back-and-forward movement until the entire area is covered. Remember to do it slowly!

Once the area is completely covered, pull the now slightly dry brush across the surface from one end of the piece to the other. As you near the edge, pull the bristles of the brush gracefully off the surface. Make believe your hand is a plane taking off from a runway. Roger?

(Do not make airplane noises if anyone is present in the room with you.)

Q I built a small cabinet out of solid cherry and cherry plywood. Then I applied an oil stain. The solid wood looks great but the plywood sides are really dark and seem to be splotchy. What happened? I haven't applied any varnish yet (I plan to use water-based polyurethane.) Is there any way to make the plywood look like the real cherry?

A Plywood, especially cherry plywood, will often stain unevenly, as you have already found out. The way to avoid this is to seal the plywood with a wash coat of shellac (one part shellac to five parts denatured alcohol), sand the wood lightly with 220-grit sandpaper and then apply the stain. The shellac, once dry and sanded, will prevent the plywood from absorbing too much stain and give you an even finish all around.

Also, a word about applying water-based clear finishes on oil-based stains: Make sure the stain is completely dry before applying the finish; otherwise it will affect the drying of the water-based finish.

Q I have a wooden mantle shelf made from (I was told) solid ash. The front is black from the soot of many fires. I've tried cleaning the soot off using soap and water and then with cleaning solvent. Some of it has come off but the bulk of it is still black. Do you have any ideas?

A You didn't say the wood of the shelf had any finish on it so I'm going to assume that it has some kind of clear coating on it. If the wood is not burned, clean the soot off using paint thinner. The good thing is, ash is a very dense, tough wood. After scrubbing with paint thinner you will know if the wood has been burned by what the paint thinner has not removed. (Of course, burning depends on how high the shelf is from the opening and how big your fires were.) Once cleaned, you can apply a coat of wax.

Q I have three upholstered chairs with wooden legs (or feet) in my living room. The problem is, the legs have black marks all over them from my old vacuum cleaner. Can these marks be fixed, cleaned or something? Nobody else sees them but I know they're there.

A I'll bet you have trouble sleeping at night too, huh? Just from your letter, I can tell that that old vacuum cleaner of yours must have had black rubber bumper band around it so that when you hit finished wood, it wouldn't dent. Although nobody ever said anything about the bumper leaving marks behind, this used to be a very common problem. It's the same thing that happens when you wear a new pair of shoes on a white tile or linoleum floor and you leave behind those nefarious black marks.

The marks can be cleaned off with a bit of #0000 steel wool and paint thinner. If you don't have any paint thinner and you don't feel like going out to purchase some, in a pinch you can use some ant spray, whose main ingredient is petroleum distillate: namely, paint thinner. Just make sure you wear gloves.

afterword

Finishing can be a rewarding practice, whether you're a cabinetmaker who knows how to build but lacks the knowledge of simple finishing, or an everyday, common, run-of-the-mill person interested in buying old furniture and bringing it back to life. One thing to remember about finishing: it should be an enjoyable endeavor. (Unless you worked for some of the people I've worked for in the past!) When you're done, you should be able to sit back and enjoy your handiwork.

After all, if it's not fun, why do it?

suppliers

For the basic finishing techniques outlined in this book, most of the products mentioned can be found at hardware, paint and home centers. Items such as solvents, oil-based stains and clear coatings are pretty common, as are brushes and sandpaper.

However, if you wish to experiment with things such as aniline dyes, touch-up materials and other "trade" products, you may want to investigate online supply houses. Shellac flakes, beeswax and oil colors ground in oil can also be purchased in most big cities from the larger art supply stores.

LEE VALLEY TOOLS LTD.
From USA:
P.O. Box 1780
Ogdensburg, New York 13669-6780
800-267-8735
From Canada:
P.O. Box 6295, Station J
Ottawa, ON KZA 1T4
800-267-8761
www.leevalley.com
I spend a lot of time in Ottawa, so I've been to the main store. They have great tools as well as a line of finishing supplies.

MOHAWK FINISHING PRODUCTS INC.
P.O. Box 22000
Hickory, NC 28603
800-545-0047
www.mohawk-finishing.com
The main distributor of finishing products to the trade. Minimum order $80.

T.J. RONAN PAINT CORP.
749 E. 135th St.
Bronx, NY 10454
718-292-1100
800-247-6626
800-654-3640 (Texas only)
www.ronanpaints.com
Ronan equals superfine japan colors, which are indispensable additions to my color arsenal.

GARRETT WADE CO., INC.
161 Avenue of the Americas
New York, NY 10013
800-221-2942
www.garrettwade.com
Carries lots and lots of woodworking tools, as well as a variety of finishing materials.

WOODWORKER'S SUPPLY INC.
1108 N. Glenn Road
Casper, WY 82601
800-645-9292
Carries an assortment of woodworking tools in addition to a nice selection of dyes, stains, japan colors and gel stains.

Any of these companies will welcome your enthusiasm — and business.
So give them a call.
Bother them.
Tell them I told you to bother them and that you need, need, a catalog and they will send you one.

index

More of the Best Books for Woodworkers!

POPULAR WOOD WORKING BOOKS

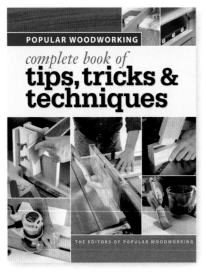

The editors of Popular Woodworking bring their best advice to the table in this massive, well-organized woodshop reference. Includes information that covers the entire craft from picking the right tool and joint to finding the perfect finish for your next project.

ISBN 1-55870-716-6, paperback, 256 pages, #70668-K
$22.99

This well-organized book offers beginning woodworkers an excellent overview of the craft and resources involved in working with wood. Learn how to use a variety of tools, understand woodworking terms, master math formulas, and execute your projects with confidence.

ISBN 1-55870-632-1, paperback, 144 pages, #70579-K
$26.99

Twenty-five projects and lots of helpful hints will help you keep your shop space organized and clutter-free! Includes six great jigs and other projects from contributing editors R.J. DeCristoforo, Nick Engler, Glen Huey, and Troy Sexton.

ISBN 1-55870-541-4, paperback, 128 pages, #70472-K
$22.99

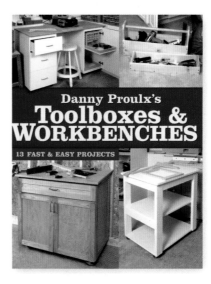

Master cabinetmaker Danny Proulx designs 13 projects every woodworker can build using off-the-rack supplies from any home center or lumberyard. Projects compliment each other and are designed to make everything that happens in your workshop easier.

ISBN 1-55870-707-7, paperback, 128 pages, #70659-K
$24.99

These and other great woodworking books are available at your local bookstore, woodworking stores, online suppliers or by calling 1-800-448-0915.